KINGS & QUEENS OF BRITAIN

The Diagram Group

BROCKHAMPTON
DIAGRAM
GUIDES

Kings and Queens of Britain

© Diagram Visual Information Ltd. 1997
 195 Kentish Town Road
 London
 NW5 2JU

All rights reserved including the right of reproduction in whole or in part in any form

First published in Great Britain in 1997 by
Brockhampton Press Ltd
20 Bloomsbury Street
London
WC1 2QA
a member of the Hodder Headline Group PLC

ISBN 1-86019-749-3

Also in this series:
Calligraphy
Card Games
How the Body Works
Identifying Architecture
Magic Tricks
Party Games
Soccer Skills

Introduction

Kings and Queens of Britain is a guide to monarchs from ancient times to the present. Each section of the book describes the monarchs of the period and some of the historical events that shaped their lives and reigns. In addition, specially extended features give the stories of some of the most famous, or infamous, rulers. Time charts at the end of the book give a full list of Britain's kings and queens from Saxon times to the present day.

Contents

6	ANCIENT BRITISH KINGS AND QUEENS 1000 BC–AD 62
	Boudicca
8	ROMAN AND ROMANO-BRITISH RULERS AD 43–500
10	ANGLO-SAXON MONARCHIES AD 500–1066
	Alfred the Great
	Edward the Confessor
14	WELSH KINGS AND PRINCES AD 450–1282
15	IRISH KINGS AD 450–1224
16	SCOTTISH KINGS AND QUEENS AD 500–1567
	Mary Queen of Scots
18	KINGS AND QUEENS OF ENGLAND 1066–1603
	Richard I — Henry VII
	Edward I — Henry VIII
	Henry V — Elizabeth I
30	KINGS AND QUEENS OF GREAT BRITAIN 1603–PRESENT
	James I — George III
	Charles I — Victoria
	Charles II — Elizabeth II
42	TIME CHARTS

Ancient British kings & queens 1000 BC–AD 62

By 1000 BC, Celtic peoples had migrated to Britain from the rest of Europe. These were probably the first people in Britain to use chariots and to ride on horseback. They were ruled by warrior chiefs. After Roman invasions of Britain began in 55 BC, some of these rulers became submissive to the emperor in Rome. Boudicca is remembered for leading the last serious revolt against Roman rule of Britain. Her story is told below.

BOUDICCA reigned AD 61–62

Boudicca (also known as Boadicea) was Queen of the Iceni, a tribe of Celtic Britons that lived in what is now Norfolk and Suffolk at the time of the Roman conquest of Britain. She became ruler of the Iceni when her husband Prasutagus died.

Prasutagus left his personal property jointly to his two daughters and the Roman emperor, Nero, hoping this would safeguard his family and kingdom. The Romans, however, interpreted the king's will as giving the whole kingdom to them, and Roman soldiers and slaves began looting it.

Boudicca, a tall, fiery-tempered woman, with a harsh voice and long red hair, protested at the Romans' conduct. To teach her a lesson the Romans stripped and flogged her, and assaulted her two daughters. Boudicca vowed revenge. She led the Iceni in a revolt, supported by several neighbouring tribes. The rebellion was well-timed because the Roman governor of Britain, Suetonius Paulinus, was fighting a campaign in Wales.

Boudicca and her army marched on Camulodunum (now Colchester), where there was a large colony of Roman ex-soldiers.

BOUDICCA

The Iceni burned the city and killed every Roman and pro-Roman Briton in it. The Britons then moved on to London and Verulamium (modern St Albans) and destroyed them too. Altogether they slaughtered more than 70,000 men, women and children.

Meanwhile Suetonius assembled an army of 10,000 trained legionaries. He lay in wait for the Britons, probably on the main Roman road between the modern towns of Nuneaton and Tamworth. Boudicca's army was much larger than the Roman force and in high spirits after their victories, but it was no match for the well-disciplined and heavily-armed Romans. Thousands of Britons were killed and the rest fled. Boudicca escaped, but killed herself with poison soon after.

'The Warrior Patriot Queen'; Boudicca's statue in London

Roman & Romano-British rulers AD 43–500

From AD 43, Romans began to settle in the southern part of Britain. The island became a province of the Roman Empire; it was ruled by Roman governors and defended by Roman forces. Roman emperors who visited Britain included Hadrian (emperor from AD 117 to 138), Antonius Pius (emperor from AD 138 to 161) and Septimus Severus (emperor from AD 193 to 211).

In the AD 120s, Emperor Hadrian had a wall built from Carlisle to Newcastle to defend Roman Britain against raids by the unconquered tribes of the north. Parts of this structure, known as Hadrian's Wall, still stand today.

Antonius Pius, Roman emperor, appears on a coin of Roman Britain

Small fortified gateways in Hadrian's Wall were built at mile intervals; this Mile Castle is in Cumbria

ROMAN & ROMANO-BRITISH RULERS

The Romans built fortified towns from which they governed local areas. London became the capital of Roman Britain; Canterbury, Leicester, St Albans, Winchester and other towns became centres of regional Roman government. Colchester, Gloucester, Lincoln and York developed as Roman settlements.

By AD 400, the Roman Empire was under attack from barbarian peoples on all sides. Roman legions were steadily withdrawn from Britain to help defend more central parts of the Empire. During the next century and a half, the beginning of a period known as the Dark Ages, local romanized British rulers replaced the Roman governors. One such overlord, Vortigern, controlled an area from Kent to South Wales.

A local Romano-British king and his officials

King Arthur, the legendary early hero, is probably based on a real Romano-British leader who fought against Saxon invaders around AD 500. The mythical story of Arthur's Round Table at his court at Camelot and his quest for the Holy Grail was told most famously by Geoffrey of Monmouth in the 12th century.

Anglo-Saxon monarchies
AD 500–1066

Saxon settlement of England began around AD 450, some 40 years after Roman rule in Britain had collapsed. According to tradition, Vortigern – a local British ruler – imported Saxon mercenaries from Jutland (present-day Denmark and northern Germany) to help defend Kent. The Saxons settled and eventually drove the romanized British rulers out of England. By AD 600, most of present-day England was under Saxon rule.

Seven Anglo-Saxon kingdoms developed: East Anglia, Essex, Kent, Mercia, Northumbria, Sussex and Wessex. In the AD 700s, Offa, Saxon King of Mercia, built a defensive dyke that defined the English boundary with Wales. Saxon kings ruled England until 1066, when William I (the Conqueror) invaded Britain from Normandy and defeated King Harold II at Hastings. William became England's first Norman king.

1 Offa, King of Mercia (AD 757–796)
2 Ethelbert, King of Wessex (AD 860–865)
3 Alfred the Great, King of Wessex (AD 871–899)
4 Ethelred II the Unready, King of England (AD 978–1016)
5 Canute, King of England (AD 1016–1035)

ALFRED THE GREAT

ALFRED THE GREAT reigned AD 871–899

Born c. AD 849, Alfred was the greatest of the West Saxon kings. His reign laid the basis for the formation of a united England. Between AD 878 and 896, he bravely and desperately repulsed a series of Danish invasions. Alfred raised 30 forts (burghs), reorganized the *fyrd* (army) and founded the English navy. He was a wise and just ruler, a devout Christian and a scholar. During his reign he promoted learning and invited foreign scholars to his court. In AD 867, Alfred married Ealhswith of Gaini, a descendant of Mercian kings. They had two sons and three daughters. The descendants of Alfred the Great ruled England until 1066.

Statue of Alfred the Great in Winchester, Hampshire

Silver penny and jewel of Alfred

ANGLO-SAXON MONARCHIES

**EDWARD THE CONFESSOR
reigned 1042–1066**

Edward was the son of King Ethelred II the Unready. His mother, Emma, was the daughter of Richard, Duke of Normandy. As a boy Edward was brought up in Normandy while England was under the rule of the Danish King Canute and his two sons. When Ethelred died, his mother Emma married Canute. Their son Hardecanute, who became king in 1040, invited his older half-brother Edward to England and accepted him as heir. Hardecanute died at the age of 25 and Edward became king.

Edward was peace-loving, very pious and more Norman than Saxon in his ways. He invited some of his Norman friends to England and gave them positions at court, although they had little power. During Edward's reign England was largely controlled by wealthy Saxon earls, particularly by the Earl Godwine.

In 1045, Edward married Godwine's daughter Editha, but Godwine continued to ignore Edward's authority. In 1051, Godwine refused to punish the people of Dover who had brawled with some Norman

Edward the Confessor with a model of Westminster Abbey

The Great Seal of Edward the Confessor

EDWARD THE CONFESSOR

visitors. With the support of two other earls, Leofric of Mercia and Siward of Northumbria, Edward promptly banished Godwine and his sons, and sent Editha to live in a convent. He invited more Normans to England and his cousin Duke William of Normandy came on a state visit. It is said that Edward, who had no children, promised to make William heir to the English throne.

Two years later, Godwine and his family returned to England with a large army and forced Edward to restore them – and Queen Editha – to favour. Godwine once more became the real ruler of the country, and when he died his son Harold inherited his power.

A portrait of Edward the Confessor from the Bayeux Tapestry

For the rest of his reign Edward was able to turn most of his attention to religion, which earned him the name of 'the Confessor'. His last act was the building of Westminster Abbey, which was completed just in time for him to be buried there in 1066. He was canonized (declared a saint) in 1161.

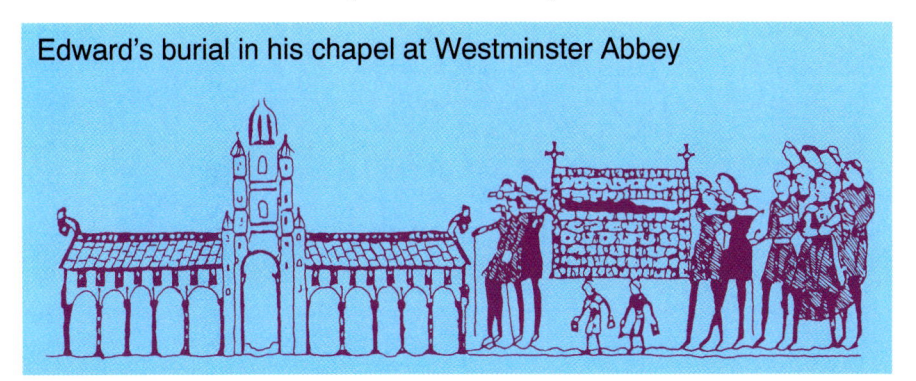

Edward's burial in his chapel at Westminster Abbey

Welsh kings & princes
AD 450–1282

Kingdoms emerged in Wales from Celtic tribal groups after Roman rule in Britain collapsed around AD 450. Their rulers fought each other to win wealth, and exacted payments from their subjects in return for protection. Most kings passed their titles on to their sons, but sometimes other relatives claimed the throne.

Three main kingdoms eventually emerged: Gwynedd (with at least 37 rulers between c. AD 500 and 1283) in North Wales; Powys (with 12 known rulers between c. 1063 and 1269) in north-central Wales; and Deheubarth (with 22 known rulers between AD 872 and 1201) in South Wales. The kings of Gwynedd spread their power by force and royal marriage during the 9th century, and often dominated Wales.

The last independent Prince of Wales, Llywelyn ap Graffydd (the Last), was killed in 1282. In 1283 a Welsh war of independence collapsed, and in 1301 King Edward I of England bestowed the honorary title Prince of Wales on his son, later Edward II. Since then, no fewer than twenty first-born male heirs to the English (later British) throne have borne the title Prince of Wales.

Llywelyn ap Iorwerth (the Great) on his deathbed, watched over by his sons; he reigned as Prince of Gwynedd from 1194 to 1240

Irish kings
AD 450–1224

In the early centuries AD, Ireland was divided into about 150 tiny Celtic kingdoms with warrior kings elected from a land-owning upper class whose main source of wealth was cattle. These kingdoms eventually formed five groups, each one with an honorary overlord. These were Munster (Mumha), with 67 known kings between c. AD 450 and 1194; Leinster (Laighin), with 68 known kings between c. AD 436 and 1171; Meath (Midhe), with 52 known kings between c. AD 450 and 1173); Connaught (Connact), with 64 known kings between c. AD 459 and 1224; and Ulster (Uladh), with 72 known kings between c. AD 500 and 1201.

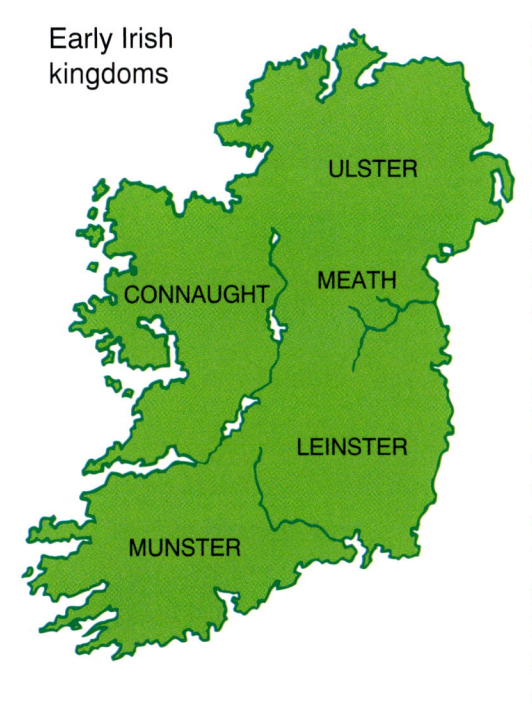

Early Irish kingdoms

Internal fighting between kings led to the downfall of Irish royal rule in Ireland. In 1171, Henry II of England ended the rule of the kings of Meath and asserted crown rights. Cathal O'Connor, King of Connaught from 1201 to 1224 and the last Irish provincial monarch, resisted English advances until his death. English rule of southern Ireland continued until 1936, when the new Irish Free State abolished the monarchy and formally became a republic. British monarchs continue to reign over Northern Ireland.

Scottish kings & queens
AD 500–1567

Scotland's first royal dynasty is said to have been founded around AD 500 by Fergus. His Celtic kingdom included part of Northern Ireland, the Inner Hebrides and Argyll. Fergus settled in Argyll and his 36 known descendants during the next 343 years shared what we now call Scotland with three other groups: the Picts of the north, the Britons of the south-west and the Angles of the south-east. Most early Scottish kings came from the line of Fergus.

From about AD 900, Scottish kings were inaugurated at Scone, near Perth. Many early Scottish kings were buried on the holy island of Iona, including Macbeth, who reigned between 1040 and 1057 and is the subject of Shakespeare's famous tragedy. In 1603, James VI of Scotland (son of Mary Queen of Scots) became the first king to rule over both England and Scotland.

Scotland's Palace of Holyroodhouse is at the end of the Royal Mile leading down from Edinburgh Castle. Initially little more than a royal guest house it was enlarged by Scottish kings James IV and James V. In 1561, Mary Queen of Scots came to reside there and it is now Queen Elizabeth II's official residence in Scotland.

Palace of Holyrood house, as built by James IV in 1501

MARY, QUEEN OF SCOTS

MARY, QUEEN OF SCOTS reigned 1542–1567

Mary was born in 1542 and became Scotland's queen when she was just seven days old. Her life was haunted by plots and murders. She had a Roman Catholic upbringing in France and married the *dauphin* Francis (later Francis II) in 1558. In 1561, shortly after the death of her husband, Mary returned to Scotland and in 1565 married her cousin, Henry Stewart (Stuart), Lord Darnley, son of the 4th Earl of Lennox. Mary became estranged from Darnley after he schemed to murder her personal secretary David Rizzio.

Darnley was strangled in 1567, probably by James, 4th Earl of Bothwell, who in 1567 became Mary's next (Protestant) husband. Suspected of Darnley's murder, Mary was imprisoned by outraged Scottish Lords Associators and forced to abdicate. She escaped to England where she was heir to the throne. Fearing that Mary would be made Queen of England, her cousin Elizabeth I imprisoned her and eventually had Mary executed in 1587.

Tomb of Mary Queen of Scots, Westminster Abbey

Kings & queens of England 1066–1603

William the Conqueror, the Norman who invaded Britain and became King of England in 1066, was first in a line of kings and queens who ruled lands in France as well as England; Calais in northern France was ruled by English monarchs until 1558. In the following pages we tell the stories of some of the famous monarchs who ruled England after William the Conqueror.

RICHARD I reigned 1189–1199

Richard I, one of the most glamorous and popular kings of England, was one of the most useless to his country. He reigned for ten years but spent only six months in England. He was a poet and musician, but it was his courage and skill as a warrior that earned him the nickname 'the LionHeart'. He was tall, red-haired, quick-tempered and chivalrous.

Richard was the third son of Henry II. At the age of 11 he was made Duke of Aquitaine, his mother's duchy and part of Henry's lands in France. When Henry II died in 1189, Richard, as the eldest surviving son, succeeded him.

16th-century woodcut of Richard I fighting a lion

RICHARD I

Richard at once forgave and rewarded all those barons who had opposed his rebellions against his father. Richard had only one ambition: to go on a crusade to the Holy Lands (Palestine) and recapture Jerusalem from the Saracens (the Arab Muslims).

A few weeks after his coronation Richard set out for the Holy Lands. The English Crusaders joined forces with the French king, Philip II, and Crusaders from Austria and Germany. In the fighting Richard was an outstanding military leader, capturing the city of Acre and twice almost freeing Jerusalem. However, there were many quarrels among the Crusaders, and in 1192 Richard decided to make peace with the Saracens and return to England where his brother John was trying to seize the throne. On the way he was captured by Duke Leopold of Austria and handed over to the German emperor, Henry VI. Henry eventually released him on payment of a huge ransom by the English.

Richard I is arrested in Austria despite being disguised as a woodsman; 20th December 1192

Richard returned to England, where he forgave the rebellious John. Within a few weeks he set out to defend his French lands, which were being attacked by Philip II. The campaign lasted five years. It ended when Richard was fatally wounded by a crossbow bolt while besieging the castle of Châlus in a petty quarrel over treasure-trove.

EDWARD I reigned 1272–1307

Edward I earned three nicknames: 'Longshankes', because of his long legs; 'The Hammer of the Scots', from his many campaigns against Scotland; and 'The Lawgiver', because of his reform of English Law.

The Great Seal of Edward I

When Edward came to the throne at the age of 33, he already had a great deal of experience in fighting from his involvement in the chaotic affairs of his incompetent father, Henry III. When Henry died in 1272, Edward was away on the Sixth Crusade. He had left reliable and capable men in charge of the kingdom, and did not return for nearly two years.

After his coronation, Edward launched a campaign against the Welsh who were raiding the border districts of England. The Welsh agreed to submit to Edward, but later rebelled, so he conquered Wales and incorporated it into his kingdom. He gave the title Prince of Wales to his baby son, Edward.

Having subdued Wales, Edward turned to Scotland, of which he claimed to be overlord. Alexander III of Scotland had died, leaving as Queen his two-year-old granddaughter, Margaret of Norway. Edward negotiated a marriage between Margaret and his heir, the young Prince of Wales, but Margaret died at the age of seven, leaving two main claimants to the Scottish throne – Robert Bruce and John Balliol. They asked Edward to decide who had the better claim. Edward chose Balliol, who acknowledged Edward as his overlord. In 1295, however, Balliol rebelled and Edward marched

EDWARD I

into Scotland to seize power. The Scots were not easily crushed. In 1297 Edward put down a rebellion by a Scottish knight, Sir William Wallace, but in 1306 Robert Bruce had himself crowned King of Scots. Edward was marching north to subdue this rebellion when he died near Carlisle.

Edward's laws aimed to prevent the Church from acquiring too much property by making sure that landowners left their property to their eldest sons. He also reorganized the national militia. Edward held regular parliaments, and his 'Model Parliament' of 1295 included representatives from towns and counties for the first time, as well as barons and Church leaders.

The Hardingstone Eleanor Cross, one of 12 Eleanor Crosses erected by King Edward I as a memorial to his beloved wife, Eleanor of Castile. She died at Harby in Nottinghamshire and her body was brought back to Westminster Abbey for burial. The funeral procession took 12 days to reach London and the king decreed that 12 crosses should be put up to mark each of the places where the coffin rested overnight.

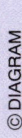

HENRY V reigned 1413–1422

By the time Henry V became king at the age of 26 he was already a seasoned warrior, having fought in a long civil war against the Welsh. He had also helped to administer the country during the last years of the reign of his ailing father, Henry IV.

Henry V's standard

The young king was a pious man, but he was ambitious for military glory and he revived the claim of his great-grandfather, Edward III, to the throne of France. The English, tired of civil war and other internal struggles, supported his decision to continue the prolonged war with France, known as the Hundred Years' War.

Two years after Henry ascended the throne he led an army of 10,000 men to France. They landed at the mouth of the River Seine and captured the town of Harfleur. Illness struck down several thousand of his soldiers, and Henry decided to march with fewer than 6,000 men to Calais and then return home.

The French *dauphin* (crown prince) barred his way, with an army nearly 20,000 strong. Henry refused to retreat. According to Shakespeare's version of events in his play *Henry V*, one of Henry's generals wished for more men but Henry replied: 'Wot you not that the Lord with these few can overthrow the pride of the French?' When the two armies met near the village of Agincourt, Henry's army won an overwhelming victory.

Henry fought a long and costly campaign against the French from

HENRY V

1417 to 1420. In 1420, the French king, Charles VI, signed a treaty recognizing Henry as his heir and Henry married Charles' daughter, Catherine. Two months before Charles' death, Henry died from an illness contracted while fighting. He left as king his nine-month-old son, Henry VI, who became a pawn in the thirty years of civil war in England known as the Wars of the Roses.

Henry V at the seige of Rouen 1418–1419

KINGS & QUEENS OF ENGLAND

HENRY VII reigned 1485–1509

Henry VII united England after the Wars of the Roses – the civil wars between the opposing royal families of York and Lancaster who fought for the crown for 30 years from 1455 to 1485. Henry was the last surviving male of the House of Lancaster, to which his mother belonged. His father was Edmund Tudor, Earl of Richmond.

Henry won the crown by defeating and killing his Yorkist rival, King Richard III, in battle at Bosworth Field in Leicestershire. He then married Richard's niece, Elizabeth of York, in an effort to unite the two warring families.

Terracotta bust of Henry VII by the Florentine sculptor Pietro Torrigiano c. 1508–1509

16th-century drawing of Henry VII as a young man

HENRY VII

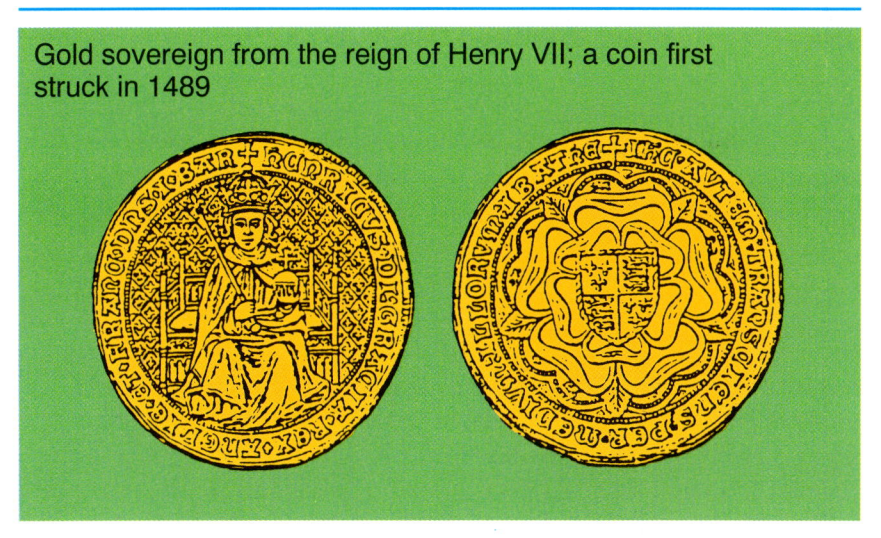

Gold sovereign from the reign of Henry VII; a coin first struck in 1489

Henry had to subdue several rebellions raised by Yorkist claimants to the throne, and by two false claimants – Lambert Simnel and Perkin Warbeck. Many of the old nobility had been killed in the Wars of the Roses, so Henry selected new nobles who would be loyal to him. Realizing that he needed wealth if he was to hold power, he enlisted the help of his Lord Chancellor, Cardinal John Morton, who levied forced loans upon the rich. The extravagantly wealthy were made to contribute on the grounds that they could obviously afford it, and those who lived less luxuriously, on the grounds that they must have savings! This two-pronged argument was known as 'Morton's Fork'.

Having acquired wealth, Henry was careful not to spend it, especially on war. When he did become involved in a war with France, he allowed the French to pay him to make peace. His only extravagance was a splendid chapel built at Westminster Abbey.

Henry VII combined the skills of a businessman with the craft of a diplomat, and he left to his son, Henry VII, a peaceful country and a full treasury.

HENRY VIII reigned 1509–1547

Henry VIII, born at Greenwich in 1491, was the second son of Henry VII and Elizabeth of York. As a younger son Henry had been destined for the church, but when his older brother Arthur died, Henry became heir and eventually king. He decided to marry his brother's widow, a Spanish princess called Catherine of Aragon, to maintain a political alliance with Spain.

Henry was a sovereign of exceptional energy and personality, but he was ruthless to all who opposed him. A succession of brilliant ministers – Thomas Wolsey, Thomas More, Thomas Cromwell – aided him in ruling his kingdom with absolute authority, only to be executed or exiled when they became too powerful. Henry became head of the Church of England after breaking with the Roman Catholic Church over the Pope's refusal to grant him a divorce. He proceeded to dissolve the monasteries and seize their lands.

Henry VIII's signature stamp, 1517

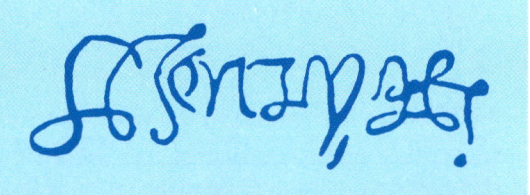

Henry married six times. Catherine of Aragon, mother of Mary I, he divorced; Anne Boleyn, mother of Elizabeth I, he had beheaded; Jane Seymour, mother of Edward VI, died in childbirth; Anne of Cleves, he divorced; and Catherine Howard, he had beheaded for adultery. Only his last wife, Catherine Parr, outlived him.

Henry, an athlete as a young man, was also a scholar, a linguist and a musician. After he had invaded France early in his reign and beaten the Scots at Flodden Field in 1513, his later policies were aimed at peace with Europe and order at home. He centralized administrative authority and built up the English navy to challenge

HENRY VIII

the might of Spain. During the Reformation, he steered England away from the chaos that accompanied religious revolution on the Continent.

Portrait of Henry VIII; by Cornelio Massys, 1544

ELIZABETH I reigned 1558–1603

Elizabeth I was the daughter of Henry VIII and Anne Boleyn, his second wife. She was declared illegitimate when her mother was executed, but her father had her well educated. She was fluent in Greek, Latin, French and Italian.

Elizabeth kept clear of political affairs during the brief reigns of her half brother, Edward VI, and her half sister, Mary I. Under Edward the country became fervently Protestant, while Mary tried to return England to the Roman Catholic faith. In 1558, most English people greeted with relief the accession of Elizabeth, who was known to be a moderate Protestant.

The new queen inherited a dangerous position. Roman Catholics, supported by Philip II of Spain, were constantly plotting to overthrow her. Her heir, Mary Queen of Scots, was also Roman Catholic although most of her Scots subjects were fiercely Protestant.

Elizabeth was intellectually gifted as well as calculating and devious. She surrounded herself with advisers, and used the possibility of marriage and the alliance this could create to gain political advantage over the Spanish and French.

In 1568, Mary Queen of Scots fled from Scotland after the defeat of her supporters and sought refuge in England. Elizabeth seized

Elizabeth I's signature, 1597

ELIZABETH I

the opportunity to dispose of this threat to her position and imprisoned Mary for 18 years. Eventually Mary was involved in one of the many plots to kill Elizabeth, and reluctantly the queen ordered her cousin's execution.

Although Elizabeth was hated by her enemies, most of her subjects loved her. When Philip of Spain sent a huge fleet (the Spanish Armada) to invade England, Elizabeth was able to inspire the country to rally to the defence, and the Armada was defeated.

During Elizabeth's reign her sailors explored the world. Her glittering court encouraged poets and playwrights such as William Shakespeare, and musicians such as William Byrd and Thomas Tallis.

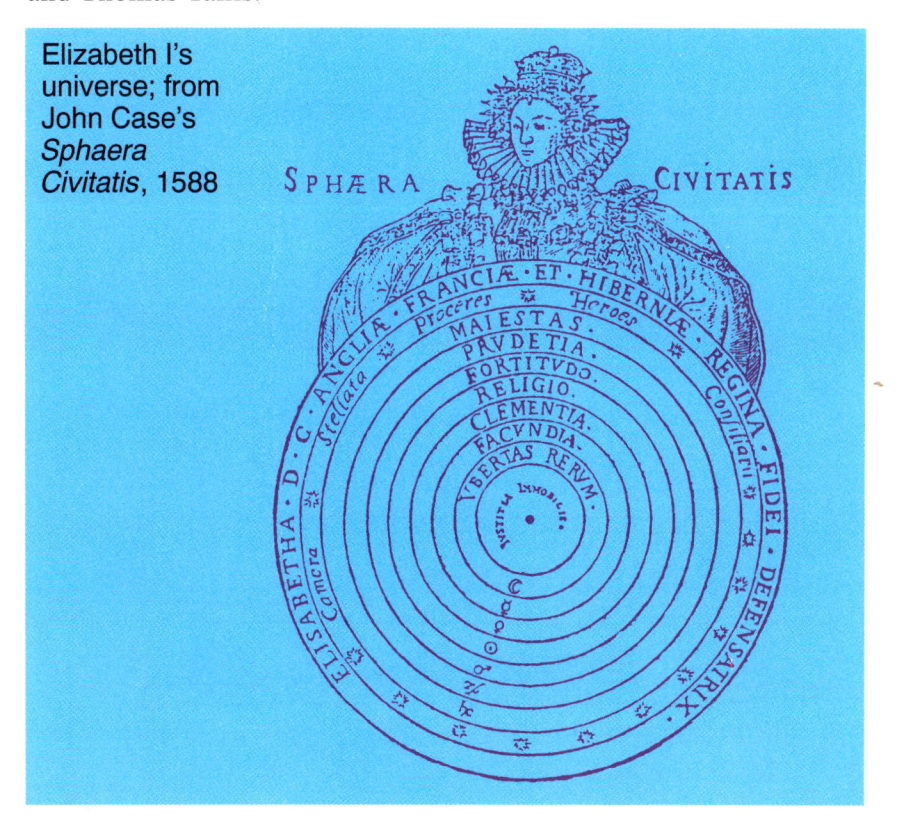

Elizabeth I's universe; from John Case's *Sphaera Civitatis*, 1588

Kings & queens of Great Britain 1603–PRESENT

In 1603, James VI of Scotland became James I of England and the first monarch to rule over both England and Scotland. Great Britain was formerly created in 1707 under Queen Anne. In the following pages we tell the stories of some of the famous monarchs who have ruled Great Britain.

JAMES I reigned 1603–1625

James I was a member of the Stuart family, which had ruled Scotland since 1371. He became King James VI of Scotland at the age of one when his mother, Mary Queen of Scots, was forced to abdicate. In 1603, he became King James I of England on the death of Elizabeth I (she had no children). James supported the Church of England. He opposed the Roman Catholics who hatched a plot in 1605 to blow up parliament and the King with it. The discovery of this Gunpowder Plot is still celebrated on 5th November.

James I is warned of the Gunpowder Plot by Lord Monteagle's letter to his chief minister Robert Cecil; from a woodcut of 1617

JAMES I

James' view that kings have a divine right to rule, together with his financial problems, brought him into conflict with England's parliament. His harsh, autocratic style of government continued through the reign of his son, Charles I, and eventually resulted in the English Civil Wars (1642–1651).

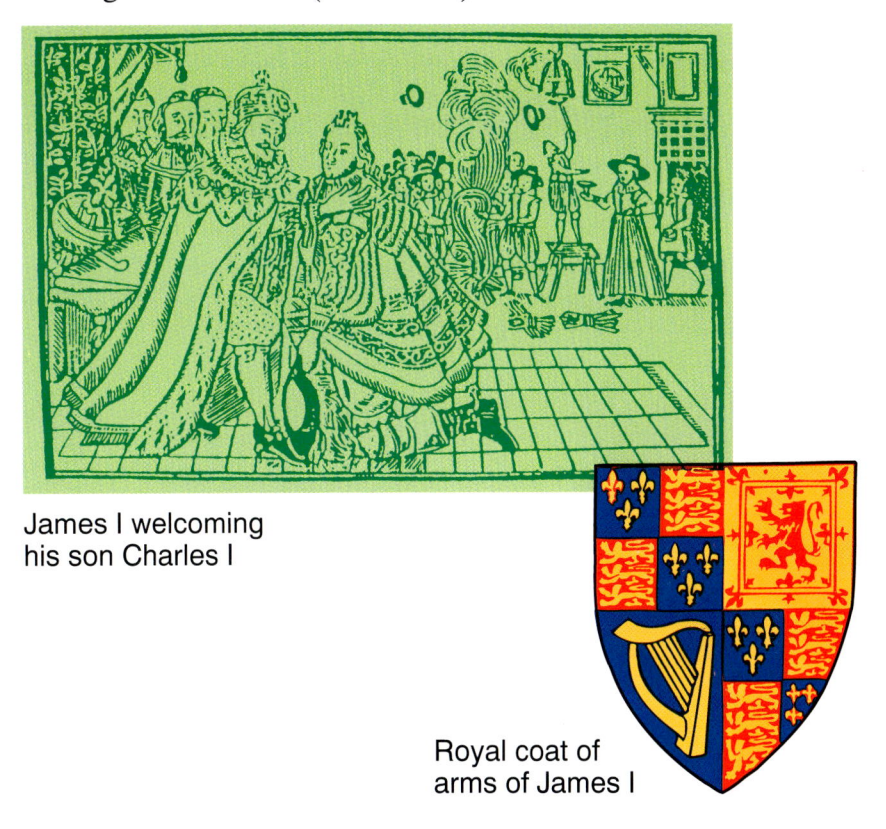

James I welcoming his son Charles I

Royal coat of arms of James I

James was a self-opinionated scholar, with a fondness for lecturing his people. He published a number of books of poetry and essays. His contemporary, Henry IV of France, once called him 'The wisest fool in Christendom'. His greatest achievement was ordering a new translation of the Bible. The *Authorised Version of the Bible* was completed in 1611, and its beautiful language has made it the most popular translation among English-speaking peoples ever since.

CHARLES I reigned 1625–1649

Charles I inherited two things from his father, James I: a belief in the divine right of kings to rule, and a financial crisis. Both brought him into conflict with Parliament and eventually cost him his life.

The new king was a little man, serious-minded, brave and a fine horseman. He had a slight stammer and suffered from polio in his youth. A strictly moral person, he was faithful to his wife Henrietta Maria of France and a good and loving father. However, he neglected the government of his country, leaving it to his ministers.

Parliament kept the king short of money to pay for the government of the country, so Charles levied taxes without its consent. In 1628, some members of Parliament drew up a Petition of Rights demanding that Charles should raise no more forced loans or levy taxes without Parliament's consent. Charles responded by dismissing Parliament and ruling for 11 years with absolute authority.

Charles I's signature

Charles I wearing the robes of the Order of the Garter, 1649

CHARLES I

Eventually, a costly war with the Scots drove Charles to recall Parliament and ask for help in raising taxes. Parliament demanded the death of Charles' chief minister, the Earl of Stafford, and made other demands which Charles refused. Within a few weeks civil war between Parliament and the king had broken out.

The civil war raged from 1642 to 1645. Charles became a capable general in those years, but his opponents, and especially their most brilliant general Oliver Cromwell, were too strong for him. He sought shelter with the Scots, who handed him over, a prisoner, to his enemies. He was eventually charged with treason against his people, and after a travesty of a trial he was executed outside his palace at Whitehall.

The execution of Charles I

CHARLES II reigned 1660–1685

'The Merry Monarch', as Charles II was known, had the reputation for being pleasure-loving, lazy and cynical. Yet he was one of the shrewdest rulers that Britain ever had.

Charles was just 19 when his father, Charles I, was executed and Parliament declared the monarchy abolished. Royalist supporters regarded him as king from that moment, but Charles, exiled in France, remained powerless while England was dominated by Oliver Cromwell.

In 1650, Charles decided to make an effort to win back the throne. He landed in Scotland where loyalist Scots crowned him King of Scotland. Charles led an army into England, but was beaten by Cromwell at the Battle of Worcester (1651) and had to flee for his life. After 43 adventurous days, Charles returned to France to begin a further 9 years in exile.

The English, tired of republicanism, invited Charles to come back in 1660. The restoration of the monarchy saw profligate spending on court pleasures and a revival of drama, which had been suppressed under Commonwealth rule. Charles was given an income that was not enough to pay for the running expenses of government, let alone cover his own extravagant tastes, so he signed a secret treaty with his cousin Louis XIV of France. In this treaty he agreed to become a Roman Catholic and support France in a war against the Netherlands. Louis in return gave him a regular yearly allowance.

Charles II's signature, c. 1669

CHARLES II

The English became involved in the costly Dutch war from 1672 to 1674, but Charles, king of a country that was fiercely Protestant, continued to find reasons not to announce his Catholicism. In 1678 fanatics pretended to uncover a 'Popish Plot', which caused so much fuss that Charles' brother James, who was an avowed Roman Catholic and his heir, had to leave England for a time. It was only when Charles lay on his deathbed that he finally officially converted to Catholicism.

Charles II's triumphant return to London after his restoration to the throne; 1660

Charles was married to a Portuguese princess, Catherine of Branganza, but the couple had no children. None of Charles' 14 illegitimate children by Nell Gwynne and Barbara Villiers could inherit the throne. Charles took an active interest in the affairs of his country, but the Great Plague (1665) and Fire of London (1666), together with his financial difficulties, somewhat marred his reign.

GEORGE III reigned 1760–1820

George III was 22 when he succeeded his grandfather, George II, as King of Great Britain and Elector of Hanover in Germany. During his 60-year reign, Britain turned from an agricultural nation to an industrial one. It gained Canada but lost its other American colonies, and fought a long war against the tyranny of Napoleon I of France. In 1801, also during his reign, Ireland and Britain were amalgamated to form the United Kingdom of Great Britain and Ireland.

George was the third king of Great Britain to come from the German House of Hanover, but he was born and brought up in England and was fiercely patriotic. He was happiest when living the life of a country squire, and his subjects affectionately nicknamed him 'Farmer George'. He was determined to be a good king, but was lacking in confidence. His political inexperience led to a series of disagreements with his governments and prime

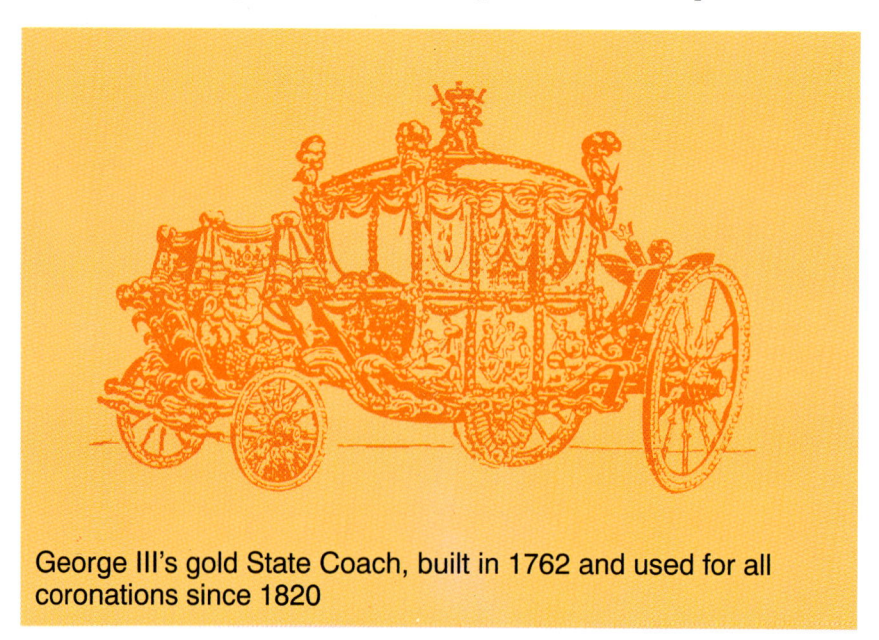

George III's gold State Coach, built in 1762 and used for all coronations since 1820

GEORGE III

ministers. In 1770 he found a man with whom he could work. Unfortunately Lord North, who was prime minister until 1782, proved to be incompetent in the management of relations with Britain's 13 North American colonies. The colonies eventually rebelled from British rule and formed the United States of America, to the king's great regret.

1 Royal coat of arms 1801 to 1816
2 Royal coat of arms 1816 to the reign of William IV

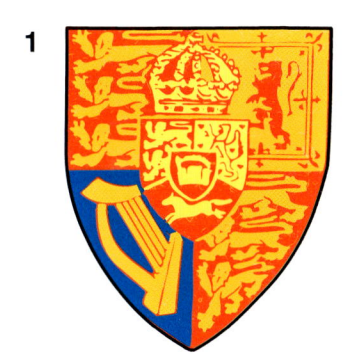

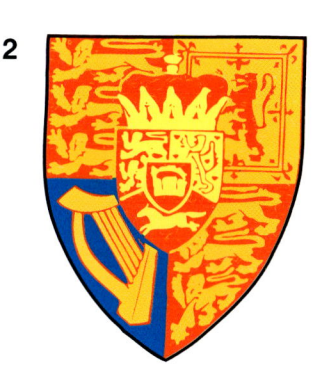

George III's signature

George also got along with the much more capable William Pitt, who was prime minister from 1783 to 1801 and again from 1804 to 1806, but the king worried about affairs of state so much that he began having fits of madness. In 1810, George became finally and hopelessly insane. His powers were transferred to his eldest son as Prince Regent. His last years were spent in confinement at Windsor Castle, where from time to time he was well enough to acknowledge his madness. His sole consolation was music.

KINGS & QUEENS OF GREAT BRITAIN

VICTORIA reigned 1837–1901

During Victoria's 63 years on the throne, Britain established a vast empire and underwent a period of enormous technological change, becoming the most powerful nation on Earth.

Victoria was the daughter of George III's third son, the Duke of Kent. She was brought up by her mother in almost complete seclusion at Kensington Palace. She became queen at the age of 18 when her uncle, William IV, died, and at once displayed an unexpected firmness in breaking away from her ambitious and domineering mother. During the early years of her reign she relied on the advice of her first prime minister, Lord Melbourne.

Victoria soon after her accession

The head of Queen Victoria on the 1840 Penny Black, the first royal postage stamp

VICTORIA

In 1840 Victoria married her cousin, Prince Albert of Saxe-Coburg-Gotha, who received the title of Prince Consort. The prince had a great deal of influence over the queen and she became increasingly conscious of her responsibilities. Victoria was devoted to her husband. The couple, together with their nine children, enjoyed a happy family life, preferring Windsor, Balmoral and Osborne House to London. When Prince Albert died in 1861, Victoria was plunged into deep mourning. She still carried out her constitutional duties, but rarely appeared in public.

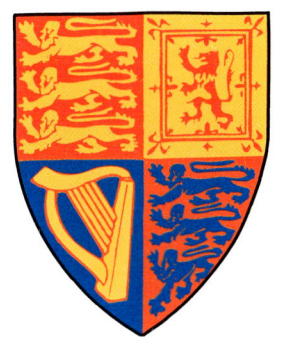

Royal coat of arms from the reign of Victoria to the present day

A woodcut of Victoria in the year of her Golden Jubilee, 1897

Towards the end of her reign, Victoria was content to leave affairs of state to politicians such as Disraeli, but was flattered to receive the title Empress of India in 1876. Her difficult relationship with her capable but pleasure-loving son (later Edward VII) resulted in his exclusion from political duties.

ELIZABETH II reign 1952–PRESENT

Elizabeth II, born in 1926, is the eldest daughter of the Duke of York, second son of King George V, and his wife, formerly Lady Elizabeth Bowes-Lyon, daughter of the Earl of Strathmore. In 1936, George V died and Elizabeth's uncle, Edward VIII, became king. Within a year Edward abdicated and Elizabeth's father unexpectedly became king (George VI).

World War II broke out in 1939 when Elizabeth was 13 years old. She and her sister Margaret spent a large part of the war at Windsor; the king and queen spent most of the time in London. Towards the end of the war, Elizabeth spent some months training in the Auxiliary Territorial Service (ATS), forerunner of the Women's Royal Army Corps. She received a commission as a junior officer.

On her 21st birthday in 1947, Elizabeth promised in a radio broadcast to the people of Britain: 'My whole life shall be devoted

Elizabeth II's signature

Elizabeth II's personal standard, adopted in 1960 to symbolize her status as Head of the Commonwealth

ELIZABETH II

to your service, and to the service of our great imperial family'. The same year she married a distant cousin, Lieutenant Philip Mountbatten of the Royal Navy. Philip, of Danish descent, had been Prince Philip of Greece. The couple have four children: Charles, Anne, Andrew and Edward.

In 1948, George VI's health began to fail and Elizabeth and her husband undertook many royal tours on his behalf. In 1952, they were in Kenya on one of these tours when the king died and Elizabeth became queen. She was crowned in 1953 and, in 1957, she made Philip a prince of the United Kingdom.

As queen, Elizabeth's duties are to act as head of state, and the country is governed in her name. She takes no active part in the administration, other than signing Bills passed by Parliament to make them law.

Elizabeth II at her coronation, wearing St Edward's Crown, and holding the Royal Sceptre and Orb; all three Crown Jewels were made for Charles II's 1661 coronation

Coin showing Queen Elizabeth II

Time charts

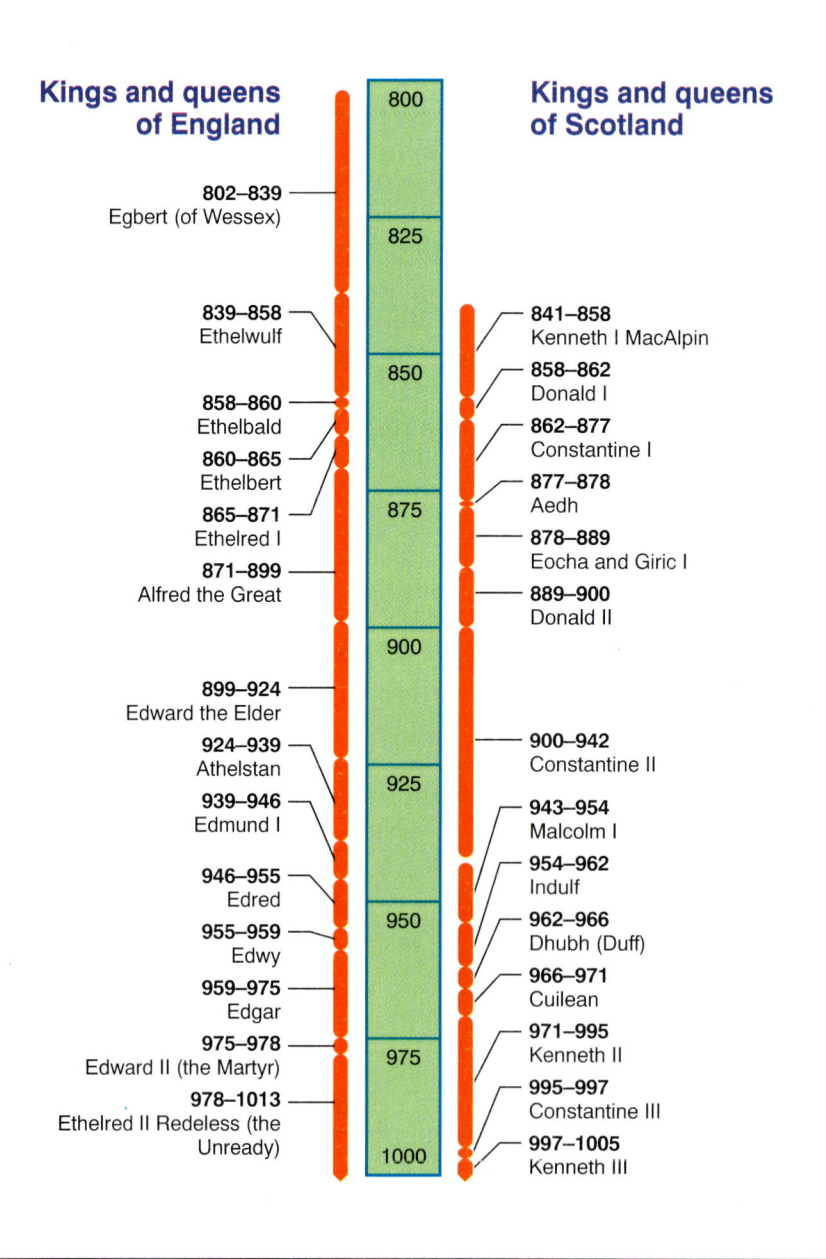

Kings and queens of England

802–839 Egbert (of Wessex)
839–858 Ethelwulf
858–860 Ethelbald
860–865 Ethelbert
865–871 Ethelred I
871–899 Alfred the Great
899–924 Edward the Elder
924–939 Athelstan
939–946 Edmund I
946–955 Edred
955–959 Edwy
959–975 Edgar
975–978 Edward II (the Martyr)
978–1013 Ethelred II Redeless (the Unready)

Kings and queens of Scotland

841–858 Kenneth I MacAlpin
858–862 Donald I
862–877 Constantine I
877–878 Aedh
878–889 Eocha and Giric I
889–900 Donald II
900–942 Constantine II
943–954 Malcolm I
954–962 Indulf
962–966 Dhubh (Duff)
966–971 Cuilean
971–995 Kenneth II
995–997 Constantine III
997–1005 Kenneth III

TIME CHARTS

Kings and queens of England

1013–1014
Sweyn (Sven Forkbeard of Denmark)

1014–1016
Ethelred III

1016
Edmund II (Ironside)

1016–1035
Canute (Knut the Great of Denmark)

1035–1040
Harold I (Harefoot)

1040–1042
Hardecanute (Harthacnut of Denmark)

1042–1066
Edward the Confessor

1066
Harold II (Godwinson)

1066–1087
William I (the Conqueror)

1087–1100
William II

1100–1135
Henry I

1135–1154
Stephen

1154–1189
Henry II

1189–1199
Richard I

1199–1216
John

Kings and queens of Scotland

1005–1034
Malcolm II

1034–1040
Duncan I

1040–1057
Macbeth

1057–1058
Lulach

1058–1093
Malcolm III

1093–1094
Donald III

1094
Duncan II

1097–1107
Edgar

1107–1124
Alexander I (the Fierce)

1124–1153
David I (the Saint)

1153–1165
Malcolm IV (the Maiden)

1165–1214
William I (the Lion)

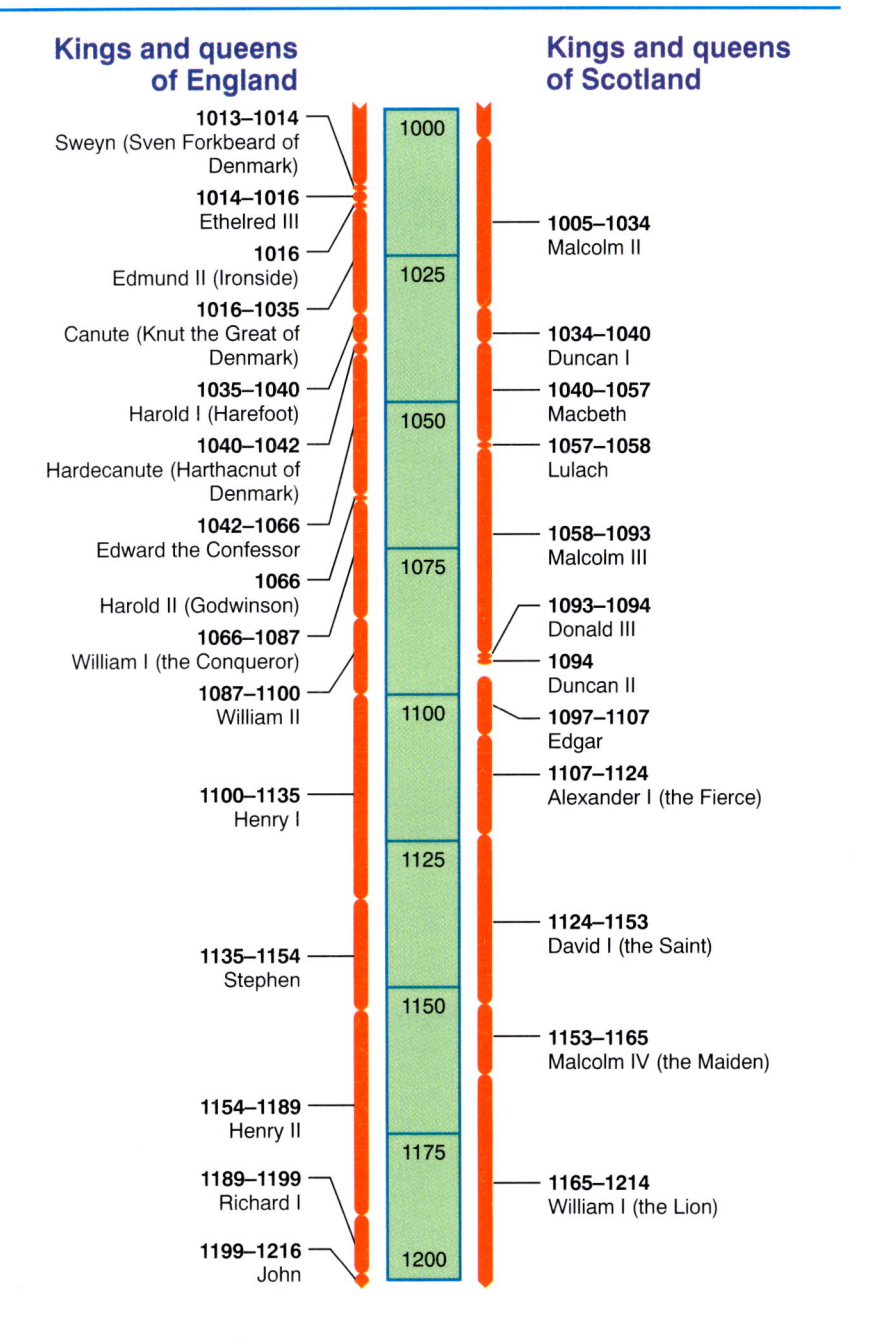

© DIAGRAM

44

TIME CHARTS

Kings and queens of England

Kings and queens of Scotland

Year	England	Scotland
1200		
1225		1214–1249 Alexander II
1250	1216–1272 Henry III	
1275		1249–1286 Alexander III
1300	1272–1307 Edward I	1286–1290 Margaret 1292–1296 John Balliol
1325	1307–1327 Edward II	1306–1329 Robert Bruce
1350	1327–1377 Edward III	1329–1371 David II
1375	1377–1399 Richard II	1371–1390 Robert II
1400	1399–1413 Henry IV	1390–1406 Robert III

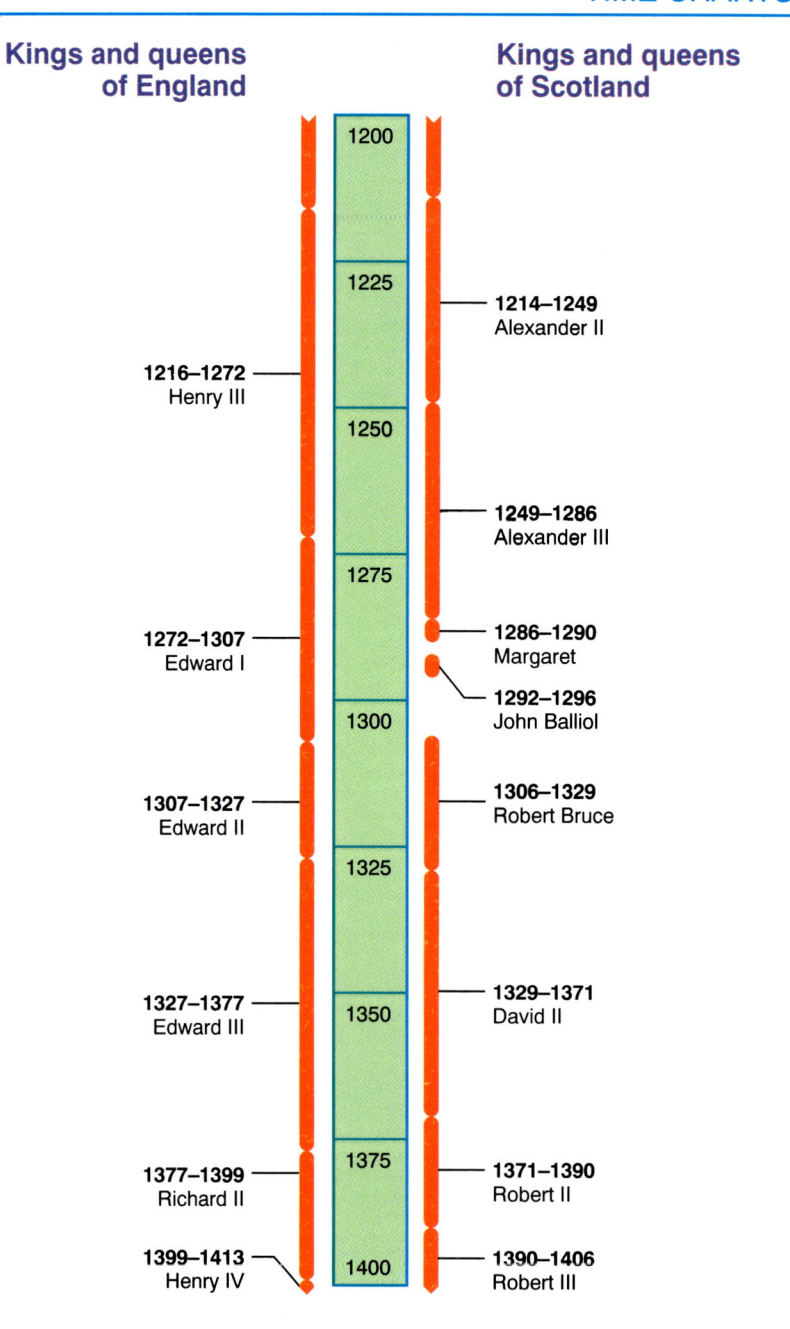

TIME CHARTS

Kings and queens of England

Kings and queens of Scotland

Kings and queens of England	Year	Kings and queens of Scotland
	1400	
1413–1422 Henry V		
	1425	1406–1437 James I
1422–1461 Henry VI		
	1450	1437–1460 James II
1461–1483 Edward IV	1475	1460–1488 James III
1483 Edward V		
1483–1485 Richard III		
1485–1509 Henry VII	1500	1488–1513 James IV
1509–1547 Henry VIII	1525	1513–1542 James V
1547–1553 Edward VI		
1553 Lady Jane Grey	1550	1542–1567 Mary, Queen of Scots
1553–1558 Mary I		
1558–1603 Elizabeth I	1575	1567–1625 James VI (I of England)
	1603	

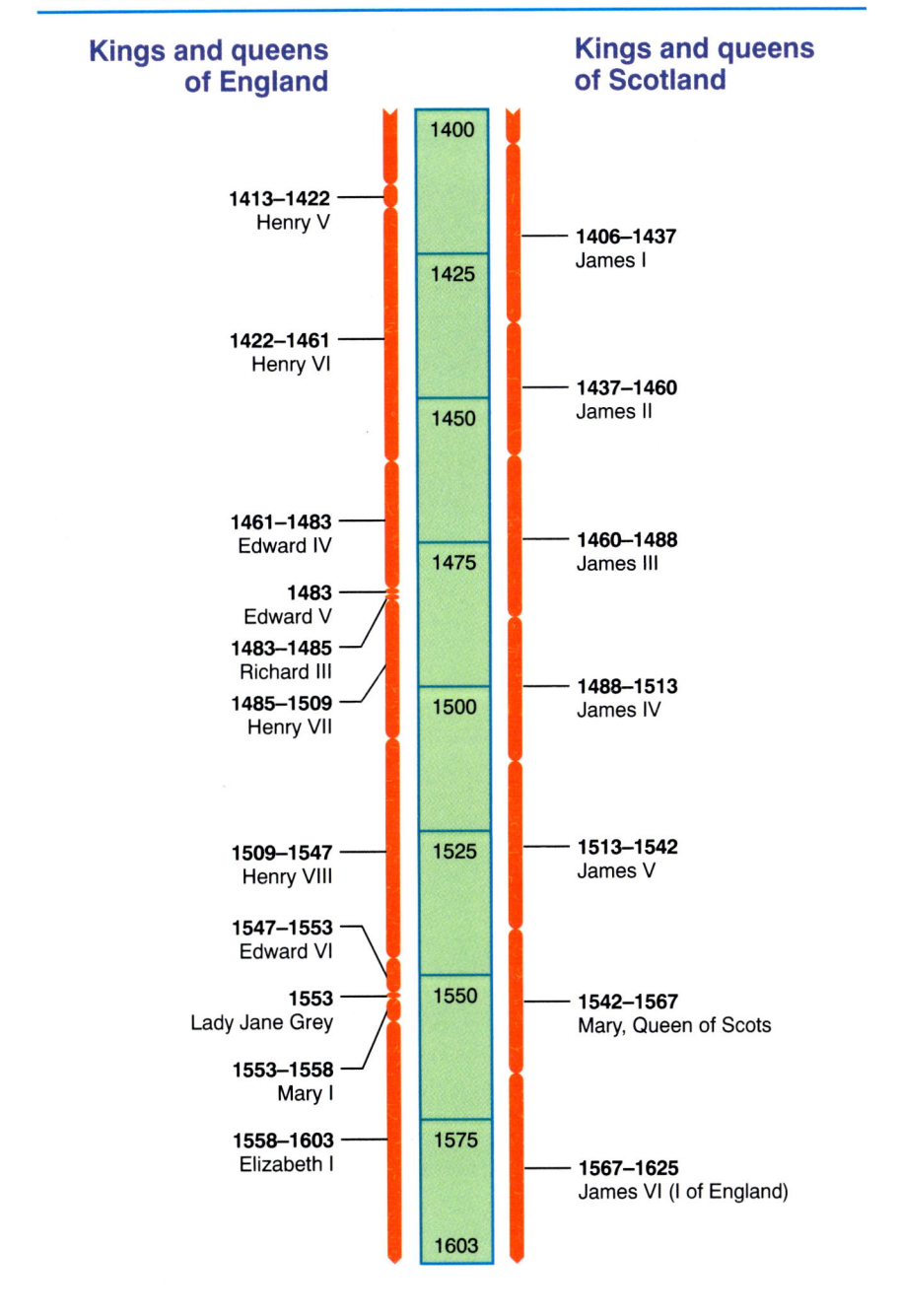

TIME CHARTS

Kings and queens of Great Britain

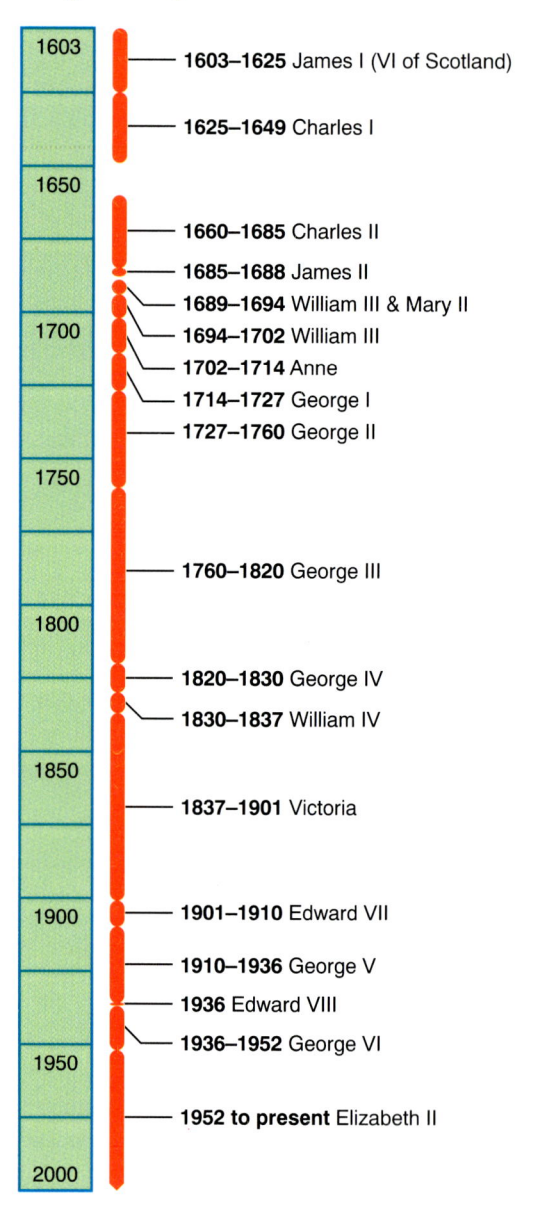

1603–1625 James I (VI of Scotland)
1625–1649 Charles I
1660–1685 Charles II
1685–1688 James II
1689–1694 William III & Mary II
1694–1702 William III
1702–1714 Anne
1714–1727 George I
1727–1760 George II
1760–1820 George III
1820–1830 George IV
1830–1837 William IV
1837–1901 Victoria
1901–1910 Edward VII
1910–1936 George V
1936 Edward VIII
1936–1952 George VI
1952 to present Elizabeth II